This book is from
Peter and Annette
to Sally with love.

Birthday 1996

THE LIGHT WITHIN

A Celebration of the Spiritual Path

THE LIGHT WITHIN

is a tribute to the many unknown people

who seek to change themselves instead of others, and thereby succeed

in taking each generation forward into the future.

THE LIGHT WITHIN

A Celebration of the Spiritual Path

JOHN & ELIZA FORDER

USHA
PUBLICATIONS

We extend our deepest gratitude to the Joseph Rowntree Charitable Trust
for all the help they have given us in making this book -
without their support it would not have been possible.
We would also like to thank Lyon Equipment in Dent, for allowing us to use
their design facilities, and Northern Arts for their continuing support
with our photographic work.

ISBN   0 9524677 0 4
Design inspired by Chris Miller, to whom we are extremely grateful
Published by Usha Publications, Dent, Cumbria
Printed in Singapore for Imago

CONTENTS

There is a Light that shines beyond all things on Earth, beyond us all,

beyond the heavens, beyond the highest, the very highest heavens.

This is the Light that shines in our Heart.

Chandogya Upanishad

INTRODUCTION

In the following pages we have explored many of the different ways in which people seek spiritual fulfilment at the present time. The story is set against an historical background among the hills and off-shore islands of northern Britain.

For centuries the rugged beauty of this northern landscape has attracted those seeking spiritual inspiration. Celtic spirituality grew from a people who had a deep affinity with Nature and, throughout the ages, the relationship with the natural world has played an integral part in people's search for Truth. From the time of the early Celtic Church, wild and remote places have been used to deepen and intensify the spiritual experience. In more recent centuries the wilderness areas of Britain have attracted writers and painters, walkers and climbers, who likewise find that the stark splendour of the mountain crags heightens the senses and stirs feelings of exhilaration and joy.

Nowadays, as eastern ideas freely intermingle with western traditions, these hills attract aspirants from many faiths.

A person's spiritual centre is the core of their Being, and everyone has their own means of reaching that inner refuge where peace and fulfilment are found. Whether priest or poet, hill walker or hill shepherd, painter or paraglider, each finds their own unique path, and the diverse patterns of individual approach contribute to the colour and vibrancy of life.

The LIGHT WITHIN is a celebration of this multi-faceted approach to the Spiritual Path. It embraces people of different beliefs and lifestyles and helps to increase understanding between faiths. Whether it is through the hills or the ocean, a painting or a prayer, everyone has their own way of finding spiritual fulfilment, yet the ultimate goal is the same - to feel at One - within oneself, within Nature, and with each other.

The Emblem expresses the universal nature of The Spiritual Path. It was conceived by Gururaj Ananda Yogi, a mystic of our time, who imbibed both the Eastern and Western systems of wisdom. Gururaj's work was dedicated to helping the movement of each individual along the Spiritual Path, no matter what their religion or belief.

Proceeding clockwise from the top - the Vedic, or Hindu, tradition is represented by the Aum sign, Judaism by the Menorah, Zoroastrianism by the brazier bearing fire, Confucianism by two tablets of philosophical teachings, Islam by the star and crescent moon. The Eternal Circle represents those individuals with their own belief systems, whether atheist or agnostic, Taoism is represented by the Yin and Yang, Buddhism by the eight-fold wheel of life and, finally, Christianity by the cross.

The nine discs rest on five golden cords, symbolising the musical staff. This suggests the idea that all religions and spiritual paths exist in harmony and are different avenues to the same goal. The flame in the centre represents the Inner Light, the Light of Divinity, or the Light within each individual.

Deep peace of the running wave to you
Deep peace of the flowing air to you
Deep peace of the quiet earth to you
Deep peace of the shining stars to you
Deep peace of the Son of Peace to you

A Celtic Blessing

INSPIRATION FROM NATURE

The people who lived in northern Britain over two thousand years ago, like those of many other ancient cultures across the world, had a close and vital bond with the land. To them, the Earth was a sacred living entity and they invested it with symbolism and meaning. It was their source of both spiritual and physical sustenance. Their relationship with the natural world was central to their lives, and it was from this that their ideas, beliefs and customs evolved.

The Celtic Britons originated from a vast moving tide of people, who occupied large tracts of land across Europe during the millennium before Christ. As these people migrated to distant lands, they intermixed with other Indo-European tribes and there evolved similarities between the many different cultures. Concepts were shared, mythical themes were repeated, deities assumed common roles and, across the world, people looked up to the stars above to find patterns of life on earth mirrored in the constellations. As the seven stars of Pleiades - the seven maidens - came and went in spring and autumn, festive celebrations were held, as they still are today in many parts of the world.

Animals and birds also took on universal significance, for they were regarded as messengers of the gods. The Bull, Boar, Serpent, Horse, Stag and Raven were all seen as being physical expressions of certain magical qualities, and they were treated with both fear and respect. The four elements - air, fire, water and earth - also had their own symbolism as these primal forces were believed to underlie the whole of existence. For the Celts, water represented divine energy so lakes, rivers, wells, and springs were venerated as sources of power. Fire was associated with inspiration and creativity, but it also symbolised the heart of the home and, because of this, it helped bring together the spiritual and physical dimensions.

Like other ancient civilisations the Celts filled their world with deities. Gods and goddesses resided in the rivers, trees, rocks, mountain peaks, the sun, the moon and the stars. They were never distant or far away, but were accessible and a part of daily life, always there for inspiration and support. The Celtic people strengthened their bond with the land by reinforcing their relationship with the deities. Through ritual and sacrifice, they invoked them at sacred places in the landscape.

Among the northern hills, groves with waterfalls, streams and a copse of oak or ash trees, symbolised harmony. There the water glinted silver, the earth was cushioned by mosses and fallen leaves, and the sunlight danced among the trees. Downstream, among some rocks and boulders, the water made a soft mesmeric sound before disappearing underground into the entrance of a cave.

Such a place would have been a meeting place between worlds - the Sky World reflecting the cycles of life, the Earth World containing the human and animal kingdoms, and the Underworld which held the mysteries of life, death and rebirth. The Celts believed that life was a continuum and they wanted to find equilibrium within it: they recognised that the different forces in nature would help them.

To the Celts the Earth was their Mother - their goddess and source of fertility. She could be either mysterious and terrifying, or radiant and benign, but by using her female powers she was able to defeat death and despair and so help to sustain life. She embraced all aspects of humankind - the aspirations of youth, the joys of motherhood and the desolation of old age, for all life was contained within her. Celtic gods and goddesses not only resided in the natural world, but they also represented qualities to aspire to, such as wisdom, beauty, inspiration and courage. Above all, the deities helped bring together people's inner and outer worlds, for the Celts sought unity and harmony - within themselves and within nature.

The Tree of Life

Similar ideas to this Celtic symbol have been found among ancient Greek, Mayan and Buddhist cultures - the two birds symbolise unity between the inner and outer man.

The Celts had a close and vital bond with the natural world - from this their ideas, beliefs, rituals and customs evolved.

Like other ancient peoples across the planet the Celts filled their world with deities.
Gods and goddesses resided in the trees, mountains, rivers, the sun, the moon and the stars.

"We came whirling out of nothingness, scattering stars like dust -
the stars made a circle and in the middle we dance . . ."

The Celts found patterns of life on Earth mirrored in the constellations.
Stars encircling the North Star.

The Underworld contained the mysteries of life, death and rebirth -
a cave entrance symbolised a meeting place between worlds.

Water represented divine energy, and so waterfalls, lakes, rivers and wells were venerated as sources of power.

I arise today
Through strength of heaven
Light of sun,
Radiance of moon,
Splendour of fire,
Speed of lightning,
Swiftness of wind,
Depth of sea,
Stability of earth,
Firmness of rock.

A Celtic affirmation

Wastwater beneath the Screes - an ancient glaciated landscape.

19

Different aspects of Nature
inspired Celtic art.

Wisdom of serpent be thine
Wisdom of raven be thine
Wisdom of valiant eagle

Voice of swan be thine
Voice of honey be thine
Voice of the son of the stars

Bounty of sea be thine
Bounty of land be thine
Bounty of the Father of heaven.

A Blessing from the Carmina Gadelica

The seventh-century Bewcastle Cross
shows Celtic knot patterns and vine scrolls
inhabited by birds and beasts.

I am a wind of the sea
I am a wave of the sea
I am the sound of the sea
I am a stag of seven tines
I am a hawk on the cliff
I am a teardrop in the sun
I am the fairest of fair flowers
I am a raging boar
I am a salmon in a pool
I am a lake upon a fair plain
I am a spear that roars for blood
I am the god of inspiring fire.

A Celtic poem

Certain animals and birds took on universal significance, for they were regarded as messengers of the gods.
The Boar represented the Land as its attributes were associated with fertility, food and rebirth.

The Bull was a symbol of strength and virility.
It was associated with heroism and courage and therefore
took on the role of god of war.

At places that symbolised harmony, the Celts used ritual and sacrifice to reinforce their relationship with the deities and so strengthen their vital bond with the land.

The Celts believed the soul was contained in the head, so an important
aspect of their culture was the carving of human figures and heads.
A group of three figures carved on the theme of Ancestral Man in Grizedale Forest.

The origin of stone circles remains a mystery, but it is thought that they were used for ceremonies of purification and fertility, as well as having astronomical significance. The Druids performed their rites and rituals at these sites. Castlerigg Stone Circle, Cumbria.

Nowadays circle dancing takes place on Midsummer Day at Long Meg Stone Circle.

When Christianity came to the shores of northern Britain, this ancient Celtic world was a fertile ground for the message of sacrifice and love, for these were themes that already permeated their culture. Indeed, the Celts already believed in an all-powerful paternal deity whose son, the God of Light, was able to mediate between worlds as a conveyer of hope and joy. So, without conflict or overt conversion, the new faith entwined itself with the existing pattern of beliefs.

The Celtic people felt no threat, and subtly adapted their old ideas to suit the Christian story. The Druids, who acted as priests and spiritual guides, absorbed the Christian teaching without resistance and gradually adopted the role of monks. The deities became saints, Celtic festivals were woven into the Christian calendar, and shrines and chapels were built where springs and wells had previously been deemed sacred.

The new faith was grafted onto the old, like a rose onto wild briar.

Celtic Christianity had its roots firmly embedded in a past where people had forged a sacred and vital bond with the natural world. It was this that helped the new faith to flourish in its own distinctive way.

The Light in the dark
The presence in our loneliness
The strength in our weakness
The guide in our lostness
He is ready to carry not only our burdens
But us if need be.
He is the mission that we take to others.

From the Breastplate of Saint Patrick

THE COMING OF CHRISTIANITY

The early Christian monks were men of courage and conviction who were not afraid to make personal sacrifice in their pursuit of truth. Many of them abandoned their homes and loved ones in order to travel to distant lands in search of God. This urge to wander, to make a journey, was symbolic of the inner spiritual journey. By overcoming their attachments to family and friends, physical comforts and needs, the monks believed that they would find lasting inner peace.

Many moved restlessly from place to place, always leaving what they knew in order to take another step into the unknown. On rough seas they were at the mercy of unpredictable weather and jagged coastlines, and on land they were susceptible to marauding bandits and wild animals. But for these first Christian monks, the physical dangers that they endured were merely reflections of the struggles on the path within.

In northern Britain and Ireland, Christianity grew and flourished away from the centres of power and, because of this, the Celtic church developed its own distinctive character. It encouraged individuals to form a personal relationship with God without intermediaries, and this allowed ordinary men and women to explore their own spiritual nature. There evolved two kinds of spiritual life: the active and the contemplative. The active consisted of doing good deeds, caring for the sick and hungry and giving support to those in need, while the contemplative involved long periods of meditation in order to penetrate the Mystery of the Spirit. Each role had its place and neither was denied anyone.

In a small cell, on a wild and rocky peninsular blasted by gales blowing in from the ocean, a monk would isolate himself from the rest of the world. With sparse rations and few clothes for warmth, he would spend long hours in meditation, murmuring prayers and recitations, as a means of deepening and intensifying his experience of God. It was a personal crusade that needed great courage and stamina, for the obstacles he was facing were within himself.

For many years the monk would live a life of seclusion, overcoming his temptations, distractions, fears and needs, until ultimately there were no barriers between himself and God. He sought to achieve a state of selflessness, and purity of heart. By letting go of his

longings and desires and opening himself up to the power of Grace, his individual Spirit was finally able to merge with the Universal Spirit - and the two became one in an experience of limitless, unending joy and peace. This was the ideal of the contemplative path.

The idea of asceticism came from the Near East. The Desert Fathers and Mothers subjected themselves to lives of extreme austerity and deprivation in the Egyptian desert and are regarded as the first Christian monks. Within the Celtic world others followed their example. Saint Patrick, seen as the founding father of Celtic Christianity, respected eastern ideas but also acknowledged the value of his own Celtic heritage. It was his understanding of both traditions that helped him to spread Christianity throughout Ireland within his lifetime.

Tales of the Saints and their deeds, embroidered with myth and legend, were handed down from one generation to the next, and these served as inspiration to those that followed. After Saint Patrick came Saint Columba who, during the sixth century, set sail from Ireland with twelve companions and rowed until he reached the tiny island of Iona off the west coast of Scotland. As he embarked upon the hazardous journey, he surrendered his life to God's will.

For these Celtic Saints, it was not ornate buildings and churches that inspired their prayers, but the cries of the sea birds, the white foam on the waves, the moan of the winds and the looming sea mists. For them it was the wilderness, the exhilaration of the natural world their own heritage - that stimulated their communion with God. Iona made an ideal setting. There, far away from his homeland and other external influences, Columba devoted himself to founding a monastic community that was to become a symbol of Christian hope and faith until the present day.

It was a time of instability in Britain. There was constant feuding between tribes, and raids and battles, strife and turmoil were a frequent part of life in the north. But, like shafts of light radiating out into this confused world, monks from Iona would travel far and wide offering their guidance and solace. Communities started up in different parts of the North and these in turn became places of refuge where others could seek help. Some were mixed monasteries where monks and nuns could worship together - a distinctive feature of the Celtic Church - while others were tiny communities where just a few people would create a sanctuary in some remote or desolate place

However, it was on another island, Lindisfarne - now known as Holy Island - that Iona's most famous daughter community was founded. Here Cuthbert, an Anglo-Saxon, followed the ascetic life as other Celtic Saints had done before him. But, not content with the isolation of Lindisfarne, he went to live on the remoter island of Inner Farne, regarded as being a wild and dangerous place.

There he built himself a cell with walls so high that his only outlook was to the sky, so that his attention would remain focussed on God alone. Saint Cuthbert became renowned as a man of profound spiritual insight, and his affinity with the wildlife of the island became legendary. People would travel from far and wide to hear his wisdom and be touched by his healing presence.

After his death in 687, Cuthbert's life took on new meaning. As Viking raids swept aside any vestige of stability and prosperity that there might have been in northern Britain, the monks left Lindisfarne taking with them the remains of Saint Cuthbert in a reliquary coffin. From refuge to refuge they carried this coffin, guarding it faithfully as a symbol of Christian hope and love. It was another four hundred years before Cuthbert finally came to rest in Durham Cathedral but, throughout that time, the Saint had helped to keep the flame of Christianity alight in the north of Britain.

May God shield you on every steep,
May Christ keep you on every path,
May Spirit bathe you in every pass.

A Celtic charm worn by a person when journeying to safeguard them from harm.

The view from Holy Island to the mainland.

During the sixth century, Saint Columba set sail from Ireland and did not rest
until he reached the tiny Island of Iona off the west coast of Scotland. Here he founded a monastic
community that has remained a symbol of Christian hope and faith until the present day.

Sunrise from Iona.

Be Thou a smooth way before me,
Be Thou a guiding star above me,
Be Thou a keen eye behind me,
This day, this night for ever.

If only Thou, O God of life,
Be at peace with me, be my support,
Be to me as a star, be to me as a helm,
From my lying down in peace
    to my rising anew.

                              Saint Columba

Saint Martin's Cross, decorated
with serpent-and-boss ornament -
eighth century, Iona.

On some island I long to be,
a rocky promontory, looking on
the coiling surface of the sea.

To see the waves, crest on crest
of the great shining ocean, composing
a hymn to the Creator, without rest.

A Celtic prayer

For the early Celtic monks, it was not ornate buildings that inspired their prayers with God, but the wind and the waves and the sea-bird cries - the exhilaration of the natural world, their own heritage.

"*Spirit of Life, wind over flowing waters,*
In earth, sea and sky,
You are there."

Iona

O *hidden Mystery*
  Sun behind all suns,
Soul behind all souls,
In everything we touch,
In everyone we meet,
Your presence is round us,
And we give you thanks.

A prayer from the Iona Community

Iona Abbey now stands on the site of the original Celtic monastery -
The Presbytery.

The Island of Iona is now the spiritual home of the Iona Community, an ecumenical body of men and women who seek new ways of living the Christian teaching throughout the world.

Looking through the cloisters at the bronze sculpture -*The Descent of the Spirit*.

Children living in difficult conditions in the inner cities are offered an experience of the countryside - The Lune Valley, Cumbria.

Noel Charlton, a member of the Iona Community, set up
the Rivendell Community so that families and individuals under
stress could be offered periods of respite and spiritual renewal.

I sought my God -
My God I could not see.
I sought my soul -
My soul eluded me.
I sought my brother,
And I found all three.

Holy Island Church now stands where
people have worshipped for over 1300 years.

Saint Aidan left Iona in 635 to found a monastery
on Holy Island off the coast of Northumberland.

Saint Cuthbert - Aidan's most famous successor - not content with the isolation of Holy Island
went to live as a hermit on the remoter island of Inner Farne. He grew to become a man
of profound spiritual insight, and his affinity with the island birds became legendary.

Inner Farne

Puffins on Inner Farne.

"Cuthbert had great numbers of people coming to him not just from Lindisfarne but from remote parts of Britain. They confessed their sins, confided in him about their temptations, and laid open to him the common troubles of humanity they were labouring under - all in the hope of gaining consolation from so holy a man. They were not disappointed. No one left unconsoled and no one had to carry back the burdens he came with. Spirits that were chilled with sadness he could warm back to hope again with a pious word . . .
. . . He showed them that both good fortune and bad were transitory in this world."

Bede: Life of Cuthbert

David Adam, the present vicar of Holy Island, keeps alive the Celtic tradition through his poems and prayers. He believes that the Celtic influence still lives on in the northern church.

On the shores of Holy Island overlooking Saint Cuthbert's Island.

I weave a silence on to my lips
I weave a silence into my mind
I weave a silence within my heart
I close my ears to distractions
I close my eyes to attractions
I close my heart to temptations

Calm me O Lord, as you stilled the storm
Still me O Lord, keep me from harm
Let all tumult within me cease
Enfold me Lord in your peace.

David Adam

Words cannot describe the joy of the soul whose impurities are cleansed in
deep contemplation - who is one with his Atman, his own Spirit.
Only those who feel this joy know what it is.
Even as Water becomes one with Water, Fire with Fire, and Air with Air,
so the Mind becomes one with the Infinite Mind
and thus attains final freedom.

Maitri Upanishad

MONKS & MYSTICS

The lives of the early Saints set a precedent for the monks and mystics of the Middle Ages, who also believed that the contemplative life was the key to spiritual fulfilment. During the eleventh and twelfth centuries, a few dedicated monks began to look for wild and desolate places among the northern hills, intent upon pursuing a rigorous spiritual life based upon the precepts of austerity, humility and charity.

Twelve or so monks would come together to find a sheltered place where water, wood and stone were available to build a small community. However, coping with conditions of utmost severity with little support from the established Church, forced them to seek help elsewhere. The monks' devotion and determination to succeed won the sympathy and support of Saint Bernard, abbot of the Cistercian house in Clairvaux, who willingly offered them practical help as well as spiritual guidance.

And so it was that Saint Bernard became their spiritual father. He advocated a life of prayer, penance and service to others and, as the northern monks had similar ideals, there developed a close and natural affiliation between the monastic communities in France and Britain. Charity was at the heart of Saint Bernard's teaching. He saw God as Love and the source of all Love, and regarded the role and duty of humankind as being to restore the balance of charity in the world. This could be done by growing in likeness to God and so radiating His Love to others. The strict daily routine of personal meditation, worship, periods of silence and service to others, was designed to eradicate selfishness and to foster selflessness.

In Britain these were more settled times when marauding tribes no longer terrorised the land as they had done in previous centuries. Angle, Saxon, Norse and Celt, now had a chance of living and working together to develop different skills within their own communities. Similarly within monastic life, there were opportunities for futhering agricultural and building skills, for material prosperity helped reinforce the life of the community and enabled it to expand.

The commitment that the Cistercian monks had to a life of discipline, frugality and manual labour assisted them in building up the monasteries and improving their agricultural land. Gradually the monks became immersed in a regime of sowing crops, rearing sheep, trading wool and managing their estates. It was not long before their aptitude for hard work transformed the monasteries from humble abodes into glorious and magnificent Abbeys and estates that stretched across the north of Britain.

During the following two to three hundred years, the Great Monasteries in the north became thriving centres of industry as the monks' success generated increasing wealth. But the worldly distractions from which the first monks had fled, now loomed large within the monastery gates. Inevitably there arose the temptation to succumb to an easier lifestyle and let go of the ideals upon which the communities had been founded. Amongst those outside the monastery walls, the vision of monastic power, wealth and comfortable living soon began to breed envy and, during the sixteenth century, the Great Monasteries were dissolved by the State.

The ruins now stand as testimony to their former glory and act as a reminder that here, many centuries before, dedicated men were distracted from their path. Where once a fine mediaeval nave stood with fluted arches and impressive vaulting, there is a strange quiet that lingers amongst the tumbled stones. Nesting birds flit about the empty shapes and only the sound of the wind whistling through the remains is left as an echo of the solitude those first monks sought.

The contemplative path was not easy. During the Middle Ages there was a flowering of mysticism as certain courageous men and women, understanding the difficulties of the ascetic ideal, determined to allow nothing to distract them from their spiritual life. The goal of the mystic is to experience directly the Mystery of the Spirit - or God.

The Yorkshire born Richard Rolle, like the early Celtic Saints, abandoned everything and everyone that he knew, in order to lead a solitary and independent life so that he could grow ever closer to God. He stepped outside convention, avoided snares that might persuade him to conform, and sought union with God through the path of Love. Through devotion to his chosen path to the exclusion of all else, selfish desires were washed away, allowing him to become elevated and transformed by the totality of his Love for God. For the mystic, ultimate union with God was consummation - an indescribable experience of ecstatic and inordinate beauty. The echoes of Saint Bernard's teaching can be heard through the poignant experience of the mystics of that time.

Saint Cedd, who trained as a monk on Holy Island, founded a monastery at Lastingham
in the seventh century where, on his death, a shrine was built in his honour.
The Reverend Christine Streeter now celebrates communion in this ancient Crypt beneath Saint Mary's Church.

Love is indeed a transforming force . . . diffusive and binding -
diffusive, because it radiates its beams of goodness not only
to friends and neighbours, but also to strangers and enemies -
binding, because it makes the lovers of one disposition and will,
and makes every holy soul one with Christ.
For the person who clings to God is one with him in Spirit,
not by nature, but by grace and identity of will.

Love transforms the loving one into the Beloved,
lifting one into the other.
The Holy Spirit's fire consumes the heart of the one it enters
and, as it were, turns it into fire,
changing it into a form that is like God.
Otherwise one could not understand the words,
"You are gods; you are all children of the Most High".

From The Fire of Love by Richard Rolle - a Yorkshire mystic, 1290-1349

At the end of the eleventh century Durham Cathedral was built in honour of Saint Cuthbert - its magnificent structure is one of the greatest achievements of Anglo-Norman architecture.

"By the glory of your creation around us,
By the comfort of your forgiveness within us,
By the wind of your Spirit eddying
through the centuries within these walls,
Renew us, and make us whole . . . "

The Galilee Chapel at the west end of the Cathedral contains the tomb of the Venerable Bede,
who was renowned for his detailed accounts of the early Celtic Church and lives of the Saints.

". . . and only the sound of the wind whistling through the remains is left
as an echo of the solitude those first monks sought."

The ruins of the Great Monasteries in the north stand as testimony to their former glory -
Fountains Abbey, Yorkshire.

The West Range served as a link between the Cloister and the outside world.

*Love is patient; love is kind
and envies no one.
Love is never boastful,
nor conceited, nor rude; never selfish,
not quick to take offence.
Love keeps no score of wrongs;
does not gloat over other men's sins,
but delights in the Truth.
There is nothing love cannot face;
there is no limit to its faith, its hope,
and its endurance.
Love will never come to an end.*

1 Corinthians 13

*And now abideth faith, hope, charity, these three;
but the greatest of these is charity.*

Hope, Charity and Faith (Spes, Caritas, Fides).
A stained glass window by Burne-Jones and William Morris -
Saint Martin's Church, Brampton.

At Hyning Hall in Lancashire, a community of Cistercian nuns follow
the rule of Saint Bernard and live the contemplative life. They offer their monastery
as a place of retreat for those seeking spiritual refreshment and guidance.

Sisters Elizabeth Mary and Imakulata in the nuns' garden.

A headstone by Rodin.

Blessed Lord,
As Francis found joy in creation,
in beauty and simplicity,
and perfect joy in sharing the sufferings of the world;
so may we, abiding in your love,
receive your gift of perfect joy and,
by the power of your Spirit,
radiate your peace
and find, even in suffering,
the glory of God .

From the Daily Office of Saint Francis

"My life is dedicated to standing before God, with the people of the world in my heart."

Brother Paschal

Brother Paschal, who follows the Order of Saint Francis, offers the Easter blessing
at Alnmouth Friary in Northumberland.

Father David Stevens, a Franciscan monk, tends the Friary gardens.

Be praised, my Lord
for our sister, Mother Earth,
who nourishes us and watches over us
and brings forth various fruits
     with coloured flowers and herbs.
Praise and bless my Lord
and give thanks to him and serve him
     with great humility.

Francis of Assisi 1180-1226

The Earth is at the same time Mother,
She is Mother of all that is natural,
Mother of all that is human.
She is Mother of all,
For contained in her are the seeds of all.

The Earth of humankind contains all moistness,
All verdancy,
All germinating power.
It is in so many ways fruitful.

All creation comes from it
Yet it forms not only the basic raw material
for humankind,
But also the substance of the incarnation of
God's Son.

Hildegard of Bingen, abbess and visionary 1098-1179

An icon of a black Madonna and Child
serves as a reminder of the links in the Church
between east and west, north and south.

"Today the spiritual life is as strong as ever.
It is just the way that it expresses itself that changes through the ages."

Sister Imelda

At Boarbank Hall Nursing Home, Augustinian Sisters commit themselves to a life of
service and prayer. Through them, the ideals of an ancient order are adapted for today's world.
Sisters Imelda and Carol at prayer in their chapel.

Boarbank Hall, a Centre of healing and hospitality, overlooks the Irish Sea.

Lord, you are great,
and greatly to be praised.
Awaken us to delight in your praises,
for you made us for yourself
and our hearts are restless
till they find their rest in you.

Saint Augustine

From the Unreal lead us to the Real,
From Death lead us to Immortality,
From Darkness lead us to Light.

An ancient Eastern Prayer

ALTERNATIVE PATHS

Throughout history it has often been difficult for individuals to explore freely their own spiritual aspirations within the confines of the established Church. By its nature, the Church tends to be structured and restrictive so that it can guide people along its chosen path. Yet belief systems and rules can suppress and stifle the flowering of a person's inner nature. Everyone is different, and each needs to find their own way of discovering the spiritual dimension. New religions are often founded by individuals who react against tradition.

Among the northern hills, where people live at a distance from the centres of Church and State, there is a tendency to remain detached from the patterns and conditions that govern the lives of others. So it was hardly surprising that during the Reformation, disillusioned individuals who reacted against Church rigidity and dogma, often chose to journey north to spread their non-conformist message. The northerners listened and took note, for these preachers were men of courage who spoke from the heart and not from texts and creeds.

During the fourteenth century, John Wycliffe spoke out against Church authority. His revolutionary words were put into direct action by his translation of the Bible into English in order that lay men and women could read and interpret it in their own homes. This was felt to be dangerous for it denied Church leaders their exclusive access to Biblical texts, and thereby threatened them with loss of control. But, for the farming families of the northern hills, the translation meant that their understanding of the Christian faith could be broadened and deepened. Their religion could be based once more on personal vision and commitment. Wycliffe also reached out to ordinary people by encouraging spiritual and physical acts of mercy such as counselling, comforting, forgiving, and caring for the sick, hungry and dying.

It was in the Yorkshire Dales that the Quaker movement also first found its voice - the voice of silence and simplicity. In the middle of the seventeenth century, a few ordinary men and women found the courage within themselves to disregard the beliefs that were being imposed on them by their own Church preachers. They wanted the freedom to explore their own ideas and aspirations.

For them, magnificent cathedrals, altars, priests and pulpits were not necessary to find God, for they believed He resided within each person. To experience God's presence, friends would simply gather together in their farmhouse living rooms, to sit in silence.

George Fox was their inspiration. He was a fearless man with a powerful message - that the source of all true religion comes from within. He was moved by a vision to come and share his ideas with the people who lived among the hills and dales, and they liked him because he suited their independent spirit. Fox talked about the Light of Christ being able to dispel a person's confusions and suffering, and convinced people that they could be guided by their own inner Light. These were words that ordinary people could understand, and Fox found a following among them. They became his Friends in Truth.

During the eighteenth century, John Wesley's prodigious horseback ministry also brought him north to preach his message of piety and salvation. He found a devoted following among the lead-mining community who struggled in desperate conditions to earn a meagre living. Wesley brought them hope that their suffering was not in vain, and implored them not to give way to earthly temptations. His message was heard and lives that had been destroyed by drink, adultery and subsequent poverty, began to be healed and rebuilt. Pious living could bring rewards on Earth, let alone in heaven. The miners, who were deft with stone, became skilled chapel builders, and brass bands were formed so that the Wesleyan hymns could be sung out across the moors. The music and singing was good for their lungs, as Methodism was good for their souls.

Quakerism and Methodism, like many other non-conformist movements, were propelled into being as a direct result of the strictures that were imposed upon people by the established Church. There were many lay people who felt that ceremony and extravagance were distractions from the spiritual life. They distrusted priests and bishops, whom they saw as coming between them and God. These new branches of Christianity allowed ordinary people once more to develop their own personal relationship with God and directly experience His grace, as the early Celtic Church had done before.

During the fourteenth century John Wycliffe from Swaledale translated the Bible into English,
so that ordinary men and women could read and interpret it in the privacy of their own homes.

The fell road to Swaledale.

"The spiritual life begins at home - in the heart of the family . . ."

Sarah Woof

Sarah Woof, a lay preacher, with her family in the farmhouse kitchen where she takes Bible study each week.

It was in the Yorkshire Dales that the Quaker movement first found its voice
- the voice of silence and simplicity.

After nine years of hardship and imprisonment, George Fox preached at Firbank to
over a thousand people on June 13th 1652. He urged them to know the living God within,
and this was the message that drew together the Seeker groups of the north.

Annual meetings still take place at Fox's Pulpit, Firbank.

Fox's preaching tour took him westward to the Cumbrian coast -
The Kent Estuary

*"Looking at sin, corruption
and distraction,
you are swallowed up in it;
but looking at the Light
which reveals them,
you will rise above them.
This is the first step of peace."*

George Fox 1624-1691

Melvin Roberts - the warden of Brigflatts Meeting House,
Sedbergh, Cumbria.

From The Quaker Tapestry, which tells the story of the movement.

Brigflatts, 1675, was the first Quaker meeting house built in the north.

"And God is as big as the Universe . . ."

A United Sunday School in the Dales brings together children from different Christian denominations.

"The World is my parish . . .

. . Christians are not so perfect in this life as to be free from ignorance - they are still liable to make mistakes. Christian Perfection is loving God with all our heart and soul and our neighbour as ourselves. It is Love that governs the heart and life, running through all our tempers, words and actions."

John Wesley

During the eighteenth century, John Wesley's ministry took him north to Teesdale.

Northern marsh orchid

Spring gentians

Bird's-eye primrose

"The Universe is always singing,
and man must learn to listen,
so that his heart may join the universal chorus."

Sarah Martha Baker 1887-1917

Teesdale has now become a haven for naturalists and is renowned for its abundance of rare plants.

"To see clearly is poetry, prophecy and religion - all in one."

John Ruskin - artist, poet and seer 1819-1900

Ullswater, The Lake District

EXPERIENCE & EXPRESSION

The rugged beauty of the northern landscape has inspired writers, poets, artists and sculptors who have felt moved to absorb it and celebrate it in their various ways. But this was not always so.

For many hundreds of years the wilderness areas of Britain provoked feelings of suspicion and terror, rather than a sense of wonder. But, during the eighteenth century, attitudes began to change. Those with a sensitive and artistic eye and a need for self-expression began to look to the hills for inspiration. To them, the mountain peaks appeared alluring, intimidating crags and waterfalls conveyed power and splendour, and rural life revealed a simplicity and charm that had passed unnoticed before.

The barren fells and unpredictable weather were no longer seen as threatening, but began to serve as an impetus for creative expression. Lakes, peaks and scudding clouds helped to awaken the senses and stir the emotions, and these inner feelings started to be translated into paintings, poetry and prose. The landscape was used to stimulate and provoke the imagination, and the northern hills became a refuge for artists, writers and poets.

Away in the remoteness of the Cumbrian fells near Grasmere, William Wordsworth lived with his sister Dorothy. They enjoyed a quiet life, their greatest delight being to spend time in their own garden and among the mountains and valleys that surrounded them. They took pleasure in domestic tasks such as planting out the French beans, gathering gooseberries, pruning the fruit trees, and, when the work was done, they would sit in the garden absorbing the subtle moods of Nature.

Weather permitting, days were spent roaming the fells, noting in minute detail how the different seasons affected the landscape and its wildlife. Every aspect of the natural world intrigued and enchanted them: the movement of a flower, the texture of a rock, the flight of a bird or colour of a leaf. And, when evening came and the sky was clear, they would wander down to the lake to watch the moonlight playing on the water's edge.

The Wordsworths were people of insight and passion who had no difficulty in recognising the subtlety and glory of existence. So Dorothy's astute eye, combined with William's intuitive feeling, allowed their vision of life to be expressed through her prose and his poetry. Nothing escaped their notice, and no moment was regarded as trivial. Their perceptive vision and powerful presence drew other writers to the Cumbrian fells to exchange ideas, absorb the landscape, and convey different impressions through verse of their own. Coleridge, Southey and de Quincey were among those who liked to spend time with the Wordsworths at their cottage. Together they drank mulled ale, ate boiled mutton, and sat late into the night discussing aspects of Life and Nature, and deliberating on their own role within it all.

For Wordsworth, it was not the beauty of Nature that inspired him, so much as the Life in Nature. His innate sensitivity enabled him to experience this as a unifying presence of which he felt himself to be a part. He believed that the secret of the Universe was written all around him - in a ripe apple, a glow-worm, silvery lichen, falling hailstones, an aged woman or a beggar boy. He believed that every experience could help to increase awareness of this Life force in Nature that radiated harmony, bliss and serenity. Throughout his lifetime, Wordsworth sought ways to deepen and enhance this mystical union with Nature and, through his poetry, to express the experience.

The vision and verse of one writer influenced another and, in turn, inspired successive generations. The same passion that the Lake poets felt for the hills and lakes, the Bronte sisters felt for Haworth and the moors. Cobbled streets and sheep tracks, snow and mist, tombstones on one side and heather moors on the other, their lives embraced these contrasts. Their home was each other, the fireside, making bread and berry pies - and their escape was the realm of fantasy and fate. Their vivid and powerful imagination enabled them to create a myriad different worlds within their own, and to become engulfed in the full range of emotions from intense passion to loneliness and desolation. The tragedy that haunted their lives did not depress their creativity but fed it, for they escaped to the furthest reaches of their minds and expressed what they found through their fiction.

They absorbed the land and let it course through their veins. They opened themselves up to the storm-filled skies, turned their faces to the winds, and let their dreams chase freedom. They drew their strength and courage from an intangible and invisible presence that they believed pervaded their whole being. The vast expanse of their minds enabled them to weave together suffering and joy, hatred and love, and life with their own destiny. Their world encompassed the heights and depths and their vision, ultimately, was one of Unity.

Since the nineteenth century the northern landscape has not only inspired artists and writers, but it has also attracted those wanting to seek refuge from daily life. Walkers disappear among the fells and mountain peaks and are prompted to reflect upon their own significance in relation to the majesty and splendour that surrounds them. There is a feeling of reverence that comes with the recognition that the forces of Nature have eroded and moulded this landscape over millions of years. This land is Nature's Church where humankind is easily humbled.

Over the past century people have challenged their relationship with Nature in many ways. To pitch oneself against the elements is a form of self-discovery, of finding out more about one's physical and mental strength. Feelings of elation, exhaustion, terror and trust, all well up as climbers scale the heights, cavers plumb the depths, and paragliders experience bird-like flight high above the hills.

As a climber stretches his fingers over a rock face and focuses on each groove and dent that may allow him to take hold, the solid grey-blue slab of granite seems to become a part of him. As a caver abseils hundreds of feet into an abyss, where there is nothing for reference but the echoing sounds of a waterfall cascading down at his side, it is as though he is as vast and open as the hole that he descends. As a paraglider flies away from the ridge, borne along by invisible air currents, he feels like the wind as he fathoms its nature and secrets of motion. The dividing line that separates people from Nature is temporarily obliterated, and an experience of Oneness wells up.

To escape to the hills is to feel freed from restrictions. To become absorbed in Nature and to experience the elements is a way of being lifted out of oneself. Wild places and changing weather help to awaken the senses and to elevate the mind. It is little wonder that over the centuries people have been drawn to the northern hills in search of spiritual fulfilment. To experience the rugged beauty of the crags and watch the gentle quality of temperate light is another way of returning to the refuge of the inner Spirit.

During the eighteenth century the barren fells and unpredictable weather were no longer seen as threatening, but began to serve as an impetus for creative expression.

Lakes, peaks and scudding clouds helped to awaken the senses and stir the emotions, and these inner feelings began to be translated into paintings, sculpture, poetry and prose.

Grasmere - the home of William Wordsworth.

For I have learned
To look on nature, not as in the hour
Of thoughtless youth, but hearing oftentimes
The still, sad music of humanity,
Not harsh nor grating, though of ample power
To chasten and subdue. And I have felt
A presence that disturbs me with the joy
Of elevated thoughts; a sense sublime
Of something far more deeply interfused,
Whose dwelling is the light of setting suns,
And the round ocean and the living air,
And the blue sky, and in the mind of man:
A motion and a spirit, that impels
All thinking things, all objects of all thought,
And rolls through all things. Therefore am I still
A lover of the meadows and the woods,
And Mountains; and of all that we behold
From this green earth; of all the mighty world
Of eye, and ear - both what they half-create
And what perceive; well pleased to recognize
In Nature and the language of the sense,
The anchor of my purest thoughts, the nurse,
The guide, the guardian of my heart, and soul
Of all my moral being.

William Wordsworth

Grizedale Forest Sculpture gives artists the opportunity of working in natural surroundings, so they can respond directly to the forest and the questions it poses. Fish and Flower by Mike Winstone.

Using natural materials different sculptors have created a unique collection of work within the forest.
The Living Wood by Anthony Holloway.

The shores of Mull on the eastward lay,
And Ulva dark and Colonsay,
And all the group of islets gay
That guard famed Staffa round.

Then all unknown its column rose,
Where dark and undisturbed repose
The cormorant had found,
And the shy seal had quiet home,
and weltered in that wondrous dome,
Where Nature herself,
it seemed, would raise
A Minster to her Maker's praise.

Not for a meaner use ascend
Her columns, or her arches bend;
Nor of a theme less solemn tells
That mighty surge that ebbs and swells.

From The Lord of the Isles by Sir Walter Scott

The magnificent structure of Fingal's Cave on Staffa inspired Mendelssohn to compose,
Turner to paint and Sir Walter Scott to write verse. John Keats, William Wordsworth and Alfred Lord Tennyson
also visited the island and were moved by this 'wondrous isle'.

Sunset from Mull overlooking the Isles of Staffa, Bac Mor, Little Colonsay and Lunga.

How sweet it were, hearing the downward stream,
With half-shut eyes ever to seem
Falling asleep in a half-dream!
To dream and dream, like yonder amber light,
Which will not leave the myrrh-bush on the height;
To hear each other's whisper'd speech;
Eating the Lotos day by day,
To watch the crisping ripples on the beach,
And tender curving lines of creamy spray;
To lend our hearts and spirits wholly
To the influence of mild-minded melancholy.

From The Lotos-eaters by Alfred Lord Tennyson

Tennyson's Waterfall near Lochaline
is said to have inspired the poet.

"As I paint I become absorbed in Nature, and experience that there is no separation between myself and the land.
  To me, Life is all Oneness."

Katharine Holmes

Katharine Holmes is an artist who works in the Yorkshire Dales and finds inspiration from the limestone rock, trees and land-forms that surround her. She grinds much of her own paint from pigment, linseed and poppy oils.

Haworth Moor - where the Bronte sisters sought inspiration.

Often rebuked, yet always back returning
To those first feelings that were born with me,
And leaving busy chase of wealth and learning
For idle dreams of things which cannot be:

Today, I will seek not the shadowy region;
Its unsustaining vastness waxes drear;
And visions rising, legion after legion,
Bring the unreal world too strangely near.

I'll walk, but not in old heroic traces,
And not in paths of high morality,
And not among the half-distinguished faces,
The clouded forms of long-past history.

I'll walk where my own nature would be leading:
It vexes me to choose another guide:
Where the grey flocks in ferny glens are feeding;
Where the wild wind blows on the mountain side.

What have those lonely mountains worth revealing?
More glory and more grief than I can tell:
The earth that wakes one human heart to feeling
Can centre both the worlds of Heaven and Hell.

Emily Bronte

To escape to the hills is to feel freed from restrictions.

To pitch oneself against the elements is a means of self-discovery -
Striding Edge, The Lake District.

*"The Underworld
stirs feelings of
exhilaration and awe . . . "*

A caver descends a 200 foot shaft in the Yorkshire Dales.

Solo climbing

"While concentrating on the rock, fear disappears . . ."

"To paraglide is to be lifted up into the dimension of invisible air-currents, to float for a while released from gravity. The beauty of motion in flight is, on the one hand, the ultimate expression of freedom, but also demands great discipline. It is a trial of nerve and skill for one always has to be ready to meet the unknown.

The inner silence that is felt is like the sky and mountains themselves.
Flying is not an escape from reality, but an escape back to reality.
It is like being suspended between heaven and earth".

Dave Elliot

Paragliding

"You work that you may keep pace with the earth, and the soul of the earth."

From The Prophet - by Kahil Gibran

HARMONY WITH THE LAND
A Shepherd's Story

Life for a hill shepherd is never predictable. Coping with the weather teaches that. Those who work on the open fell are only too aware of Nature's whims and temperaments, and their attitude to the land is one of awe and respect. There are few who have not been caught out in blizzards, disorientated in mists, whipped across the face by wind and rain, and burned by the summer sun. Over the years, experience tells that life on the fell is always uncertain.

The shepherd will pause for a while on his way to gather sheep in order to spend time watching the land so that he can understand its moods. In the early morning, when the air is cool and the sun is rising behind a veil of haze, the sky is bathed with a wash of pinks and yellows. At first, there is not enough warmth to clear the valley mist, and it lingers uncertainly above the lake. But, as a breeze stirs, wisps of vapour spiral upward and swirl around, making the surrounding hills, trees and white-washed cottages come and go from view. There is a sense of mystery about the place. At such moments of poignant beauty, the land inspires.

But it is not just a momentary experience that gives depth to the shepherd's life. It is the feeling that, through this land, he is linked to other generations that span thousands of year. Now it is his turn to take care of the hills, as his forebears have done before him. As he follows the well-worn tracks across the fell, he is aware of the ancient Celtic roots, of the time when the monks managed large flocks of sheep on their extensive estates and, more recently, how shepherds have struggled on alone to make a living from the rough terrain.

During the past millennium the landscape has changed significantly. Man has re-ordered it to suit his own needs. There used to be vast tracts of forest that stretched across the fells, and wild animals roamed free, but sheep and agriculture have put an end to the oak and willow trees. Now, there are only a few rowans left clinging to the crags and, on the tops, there is nothing but an open expanse of barren fell.

Isolated farmhouses, sparse population and little contact with the outside world, used to mean that the shepherd endured long periods of solitude. But that has changed too. Nowadays he shares the fell with visitors, who come in increasing numbers to seek temporary refuge from their urban lives. There are ramblers, back-packers, climbers, campers, family parties, everyone with their own idea of how to enjoy the fell.

The hills are different for the shepherd. They are his life, his permanent reality. For him they are no refuge. Every day he has to face those familiar outlines that stretch across the sky, that artists paint and poets write about, knowing that he has to make those hills work for him. And, over the years, the hills and mountain crags rarely cease to test his strengths and frailties. The farmstead is often situated in a bleak place where there is little shelter. Gusts of wind can frequently buffet the house and, even on a June day when the sun is high in the sky, a breeze can persistently blow in off the fell. There are blizzards at lambing-time, and rain at haytime, aging farm machinery constantly fails, sheep prices vary as much as the weather, and there are endless changes in agricultural policy.

Yet, despite the difficulties, there is an ethereal quality to northern light that entrances the shepherd.   This is his solace. As the days shorten and autumn sets in, the lower arc of the sun leaves long shadows and soft tones. From the fell top, he can see the bracken turn a golden brown, the grasses yellow and the hills merge into one another in gradients of subtle shades.   This is a shepherd's privilege - to watch the changing light throughout the seasons of the year . . . from the day's beginning until the day's end.

The fell has many changing faces: wild, uplifting, desolate, bitter, gentle, but underlying these different elements there is a permanence about this landscape that inspires and invigorates.   The shepherd feels connected to the land. It offers him stability and, because of this, he is able to accept uncertainty.   He knows that the hills will never cease to challenge him - but it is from them that he draws his strength. They are his life, his work, and his inspiration.

For the shepherd the hills are his life, his permanent reality - he has to make the land work for him.

Watendlath, The Lake District

Psalm 1

Blessed are the man and the woman
who have grown beyond their greed
and have put an end to their hatred
and no longer nourish illusions.
But they delight in the way things are
and keep their hearts open, day and night.
They are like trees planted near flowing rivers,
which bear fruit when they are ready.
Their leaves will not fall or wither.
Everything they do will succeed.

Herbert and Ennis Bentham

"I often feel like that woman in t' Bible - the one that goes for more oil from t' vessel and
there's only just enough to make the next batch of bread . . . yes, I often feel like her . . . "

In winter the farmhouse can feel isolated and bleak.

The sacred Three
To save,
To shield,
To surround
The hearth,
The house,
The household,
This eve,
This night,
Oh! this eve,
This night
And every night,
Each single night.

A Household blessing
from the Hebrides

The kitchen is a place of warmth and refuge.

Those who work among the hills are only too aware of Nature's whims and temperaments -
their attitude to the land is one of awe and respect.

A stretch of fine weather during haytime means that family and friends pull together until the work is done.

Orphaned lambs.

Bewildered lambs after April snow.

A shepherd's life is dedicated to caring for the animals.

"The hill shepherd must be ever-vigilant, watching the weather as he watches over his sheep."

Ascending fast with his long pole in hand,
Or winding in and out among the crags.
What need to follow him through what he does
Or sees in his day's march? He feels himself
In those vast regions where his service is
A Freeman; wedded to his life of hope
And hazard, and hard labour interchang'd
With that majestic indolence so dear
To native Man. A rambling schoolboy, thus
Have I beheld him, without knowing why
Have felt his presence in his own domain,
As of a Lord and Master; or a Power
Or Genius, under Nature, under God,
Presiding.

From The Shepherd by William Wordsworth

The Northern Pennines

Give the milk
And thou'lt have the blessing
Of the King of the earth,
The King of the sea,
The King of heaven,
The King of the angels,
The King of the City.

Give the milk my treasure,
Give quietly, with steady flow,
Give the milk, my treasure,
With steady flow and calmly.

A Gaelic Blessing

Traditions and skills are passed on from one generation to the next.

A sense of unity develops within the family as they work together.

It is the shepherd's privilege to watch the changing light throughout the seasons of the year . . . from the day's beginning until the day's end.

I see the sunlight
On the hills of my Father's house
Showing me the foundation
Of my free salvation.

From the Carmina Gadelica

*"In stillness we not only find our individual self, but we find our Universal Self,
for the extent of every man is as vast as the Universe.
The entire Universe is within each and everyone. It is only when the
individuality merges away in Universality that we become boundless and timeless
and experience that all is One."*

Gururaj Ananda, mystic 1932-1988

THE PATH TO UNITY

A Spiritual Path is an individual expression of oneself. Priest or poet, hill shepherd or hill walker, everyone has their own way of finding inner fulfilment.

As eastern ideas increasingly entwine themselves with western beliefs, there is now the opportunity of drawing upon a host of different traditions from across the world, to find the spiritual ideal that is most suited to one's nature. Some people believe in the Personal God that takes human form, while others believe in an Impersonal God that lies beyond all existence. For some, God exists within everyone, while for others there is no God at all. Different conceptions of God abound but, for many, having an ideal is crucial to the process of seeking.

The spiritual journey is described in many ways through different religions, in sacred texts as well as through myth, art and poetry. Hindus speak of a path of Self-Realisation that culminates in mergence with the Brahman - the universal, infinite, transcendent Reality. Buddhists regard Nirvana, the Ultimate Truth, as the final state of Liberation, while Taoists seek harmony with the Tao, the eternal force that pervades the Universe. The Christian ideal is expressed in the concept of the Holy Trinity - the Father, the Son and the Holy Spirit - Three in One.

The path of Yoga, or Way of Union, is one of the world's oldest religions. It has been refined over thousands of years in the Indian sub-continent under the guidance of many different mystics. A variety of spiritual practices, combined with a system of ethical conduct, have the effect of freeing the mind from impressions that cloud awareness and prevent an individual from experiencing their Real Self. Meditation practices allow the mind to return to a point of stillness so that a person can be released from the conditions that cause suffering. It is then that the true nature of the Universal Self can be realised.

The concept of Taoism is associated with Lao-Tzu, who lived about 2,600 years ago in China. The Tao is regarded as too subtle to be contained in any one definition, because the Tao lies beyond existence. Yet, everything has Tao within it. The duality of creation is expressed by the two forces of yin and yang. The yin energy is the potential, creative, feminine force, and the yang energy is expansive, active and masculine. Although they are One in essence, when manifest they become two and depict the eternal interplay of Nature. For a Taoist the art of life is to attain a state of absolute harmony, whereby these two opposing forces are brought to a point of balance. A person is then restored to a state of naturalness, and the Light of Perfection, or the Tao, is able to shine through the individual self.

One hundred years after Lao-Tzu, the Buddha was born in North India. The Buddha, also known as the Awakened One, taught that everyone has the potential of achieving Buddha-hood through their own personal endeavour. Central to Buddhist teaching is the idea that suffering arises from the illusory world that is created around the concept of the ego. The purpose of Buddhist practice, based upon the three pillars of ethical conduct, wisdom and meditation, is not to destroy the ego but to disentangle it from the patterns of thought, emotion and fantasy, that continue to re-create it. As someone progresses along the path, consciousness becomes calmer and clearer, until it is eventually restored to the vastness and freedom of its True Reality. This is Nirvana, or Enlightenment, when a person is awakened from the pain and confusion of life's dream, to experience final release, or Liberation.

Nowadays aspirants from many different faiths migrate to the northern hills, and ideas from east, west, north and south intertwine and merge. Today a student of Tai Chi may also practise meditation, attend Quaker meeting, take to the hills for spiritual refreshment, and pursue a code of ethical conduct that suits his or her own particular conscience. Followers of Buddhism, Yoga, Tai Chi, Baha'i and Sufism, now live side by side with those from different Christian traditions, and each inspires the other.

Sometimes people choose to live for a number of years within a community or monastery, to enable spiritual experience to be deepened away from the distractions of worldly living. These monastic centres are oases of calm that also offer temporary sanctuary to those in need, just as they did hundreds of years ago within the early Celtic Christian Church.

Occasionally these monasteries assume unique roles. Kagyu Samye Ling - situated in the Scottish lowlands - was founded in 1967 and was the very first Tibetan Monastery to be built in the west. Not only has it become a centre dedicated to the preservation of Tibetan religion, culture, medicine and art, but it is also at the hub of international humanitarian activities and a driving force behind Inter faith dialogue. Its brightly coloured temple, hidden deep among the pine forests and surrounded by prayer flags that wave in the wind, attracts people from all over the world who wish to deepen their experience of Tibetan Buddhism's central philosophy - namely that through applying the power of compassion, every aspect of life may be improved.

Likewise the Findhorn Foundation has its home in north-east Scotland, where its international community is committed to the ideal of holistic education, based upon the principle of living in harmony with the environment and each other. Founded by Peter and Eileen Caddy and Dorothy Maclean in 1962, it first became known for its work with plants and vegetables and communing with subtle energies in Nature, and it is now a pioneering centre that continually seeks new ways of increasing environmental knowledge and awareness.

In the west today teachers offering all kinds of spiritual practices and means of self-development abound, and it is left to individuals to choose the means of spiritual unfoldment that suits their particular nature. It is through Inter-faith dialogue, prayer and meditation that understanding deepens, dividing lines disappear, and people are brought closer to each other through the process of sharing. For, at the heart of all the religious traditions, is the teaching of love and compassion, tolerance and understanding.

As never before, people now have the freedom to discover their own particular way of finding spiritual fulfilment. The diversity of individual approach adds to the colour and vibrancy of life and is to be celebrated and enjoyed, for the ideal of each person is the same . . to realise inner freedom, peace and boundless Love.

Statue of Sakyamuni Buddha
at the Samye Ling Tibetan Centre in Scotland.

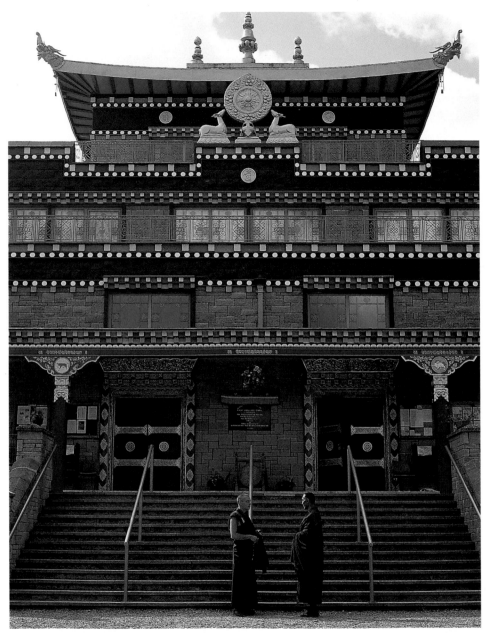

Samye Ling - situated among the Scottish lowlands in Eskdalemuir - was the first Tibetan Buddhist monastery to be built in the West.

Buddhism has been a major world religion for over 2,500 years. It is rooted in
the principles of non-violence, universal loving kindness, peace and forbearance.

Prayers in the Shrine Room at Samye Ling.

Every being in the Universe
is an expression of the Tao.
It springs into existence,
unconscious, perfect, free,
takes on a physical body,
lets circumstances complete it.
That is why every being
spontaneously honours the Tao.

The Tao gives birth to all beings,
nourishes them, maintains them,
cares for them, comforts them, protects them,
takes them back to Itself,
creating without possessing,
acting without expecting,
guiding without interfering.
That is why love of the Tao
is in the very nature of things.

Lao Tzu

Through a series of slow and controlled movements, the practice of Tai Chi is
a way of attaining balance between the physical, mental and spiritual planes.

The word Yoga means 'Union', and its ideal is to allow the individual consciousness to return to a state of Universality. A series of physical and mental disciplines is used to achieve this goal.

'Salute to the Sun' - the practice of Vinyasa Yoga.

O life-giving sun,
off-spring of the Lord of Creation,
solitary seer of heaven!
Spread thy Light,
and withdraw thy blinding splendour
That I may behold thy radiant form -
That cosmic Spirit which lies at thy heart,
For I myself am That.

Isha Upanishad

Some people find that taking care of the environment
becomes their means of spiritual unfoldment.

In the cherry blossom's shade
There is no such thing
as a stranger.

Issa, a Japanese poet 1763-1827

The Findhorn Foundation in north-east Scotland is recognized internationally
as a centre for environmental and holistic education.
A few moments of meditation before work begins in the gardens.

"At Findhorn we learn to work with love, understand the concept of service,
and build self-discipline, so that we may transform conflict into co-operation and support.
We celebrate the Divinity within all Life - and are dedicated to creating
a more positive future for our planet."

Findhorn is a pioneering centre that seeks new ways of increasing environmental knowledge and awareness. An ecological housing project has been initiated to further the principles of energy conservation and waste recycling.

A house is being built using a recycled whisky vat.

"*There can be a moment in healing when there is perfect balance*
and all distinction between physician and patient, healer and wounded disappears.
It is at this point that something else can enter and both are transported to a place of mystery.
Part of us yearns to return to this place because it is here that we are made whole."

Mark Young - osteopath and Sufi

SUFI POEMS

I sought solitude
with my loved one
yet find there is no one here
but myself.
And if there were
'someone else'
I should not in truth
have attained her.

Fakhruddin Iraqui

Those slain by the dagger of submission,
Each moment get a new life from the Unseen.

Ahmad Jam

*U*niversal or Divine Love is not an emotion but a state of Being.
Love in this form is limitless needing no expansion or development, for it is
Self-luminous and Self-existent. It cannot be defined, only experienced.
It springs from the super-conscious level and - when realised - this Divine Love
pervades our whole being, flows out spontaneously and touches all objects,
enlivening them with its power.

Love is neither born nor created - it merely has to be discovered.
Spiritual and meditation practices help break down the barriers that restrict the Heart,
so that the Light of Love can shine through in its fullest glory.
The ability to experience this Love forms the basis of all spiritual unfoldment.

From the teachings of Gururaj Ananda, 1932-1988

Meditation allows the mind to become still, so that stresses
can be dissolved and the Light of Divinity can shine through.

At the Samye Ling Tibetan Centre prayers of peace are sent out to the world.

The Mani prayer wheel turns continuously.

"Although I have found my own Buddhist religion helpful in generating love and compassion, I am convinced that these qualities can be developed by anyone, with or without religion. I further believe that all religions pursue the same goals: those of cultivating goodness and bringing happiness to all human beings. Though the means might appear different, the ends are the same.

I believe all religions are an individual decision.
And I believe the basis of all religions is love, compassion and human affection. All the major religions carry this same message and bear witness to the basic goodness within a human being."

His Holiness The Dalai Lama

We would like to acknowledge and thank the following authors, editors, translators and publishers who have allowed us to use excerpts from their works:

Pages 6, 46, 133	The Upanishads - Sacred texts of the Hindu religion Translated by Juan Mascaro • Penguin
Pages 21, 32, 35, 111, 118	The Celtic Vision: Prayers and Blessings from the Outer Hebrides - Selections from the Carmina Gadelica Edited by Esther de Waal • Darton, Longman and Todd Ltd
Pages 36, 38, 53	Prayers and Blessings from The Iona Community
Pages 40, 45	The Edge of Glory - Prayers in the Celtic Tradition David Adam • Triangle/SPCK
Pages 109, 130	The Enlightened Heart - An Anthology of Sacred Poetry Edited and translated by Stephen Mitchell • Harper and Row
Page 16	From the writings of Rumi - Sufi mystic and poet, 1207-1273
Pages 122, 140	From Darkness to Light - A Selection of talks by Gururaj Ananda Yogi. Edited by Vidya Anderson and Roopa Morosani

The Emblem (page 9) is the Registered Trade Mark of the Gururaj Ananda Foundation. We are grateful to them for allowing us the reproduction rights.

SELECTED BIBLIOGRAPHY

Celtic Gods Celtic Goddesses	R. J. Stewart
The Celtic Alternative	Shirley Toulson
The Celts	Frank Delaney
Columba	Ian Finlay
Lives of the Saints: Cuthbert	The Venerable Bede
The Christians	Bamber Gascoigne
A History of Christian Spirituality	Edited by Louis Bouyer
The World's Religions	Ninian Smart
Mysticism in English Literature	Caroline Spurgeon
Mysticism and Philosophy	W. Stace
The Three Brontes	May Sinclair
Living Buddhism	Andrew Powell
Celtic Art	George Bain

We are most grateful for the hospitality we received while photographing at the following places:-

The Franciscan Friary, Alnmouth, Northumberland - Boarbank Hall, Grange-over-Sands, Cumbria - The Monastery of Our Lady of Hyning, Carnforth, Lancashire - Samye Ling, Eskdalemuir, Scotland - The Findhorn Foundation, and The Meeting House in Kendal, which displays The Quaker Tapestry.